PRINCE
AMONG
SLAVES

For my beloved briouat,
Zayn and Zakaria.
—N. H. S.
To my parents,
who encouraged me.
—A. R.

NANCY PAULSEN BOOKS
An imprint of Penguin Random House LLC
1745 Broadway, New York, New York 10019

First published in the United States of America by Nancy Paulsen Books, an imprint of Penguin Random House LLC, 2025
Text copyright © 2025 by Naheed Hasnat • Illustrations copyright © 2025 by Anna Rich • Penguin supports copyright. Copyright fuels creativity, encourages diverse voices, promotes free speech, and creates a vibrant culture. Thank you for buying an authorized edition of this book and for complying with copyright laws by not reproducing, scanning, or distributing any part of it in any form without permission. You are supporting writers and allowing Penguin to continue to publish books for every reader. • Nancy Paulsen Books and colophon are trademarks of Penguin Random House LLC. • The Penguin colophon is a registered trademark of Penguin Books Limited. • Visit us online at PenguinRandomHouse.com. • Library of Congress Cataloging-in-Publication Data is available. • Manufactured in China • ISBN 9781984816986 • 10 9 8 7 6 5 4 3 2 1 • TOPL • Edited by Stacey Barney • Design by Eileen Savage • Text set in Adobe Caslon Pro • The artwork was created using Golden Soflat acrylic paint, which dries without a shine, and Arches watercolor paper. • The publisher does not have any control over and does not assume any responsibility for author or third-party websites or their content.

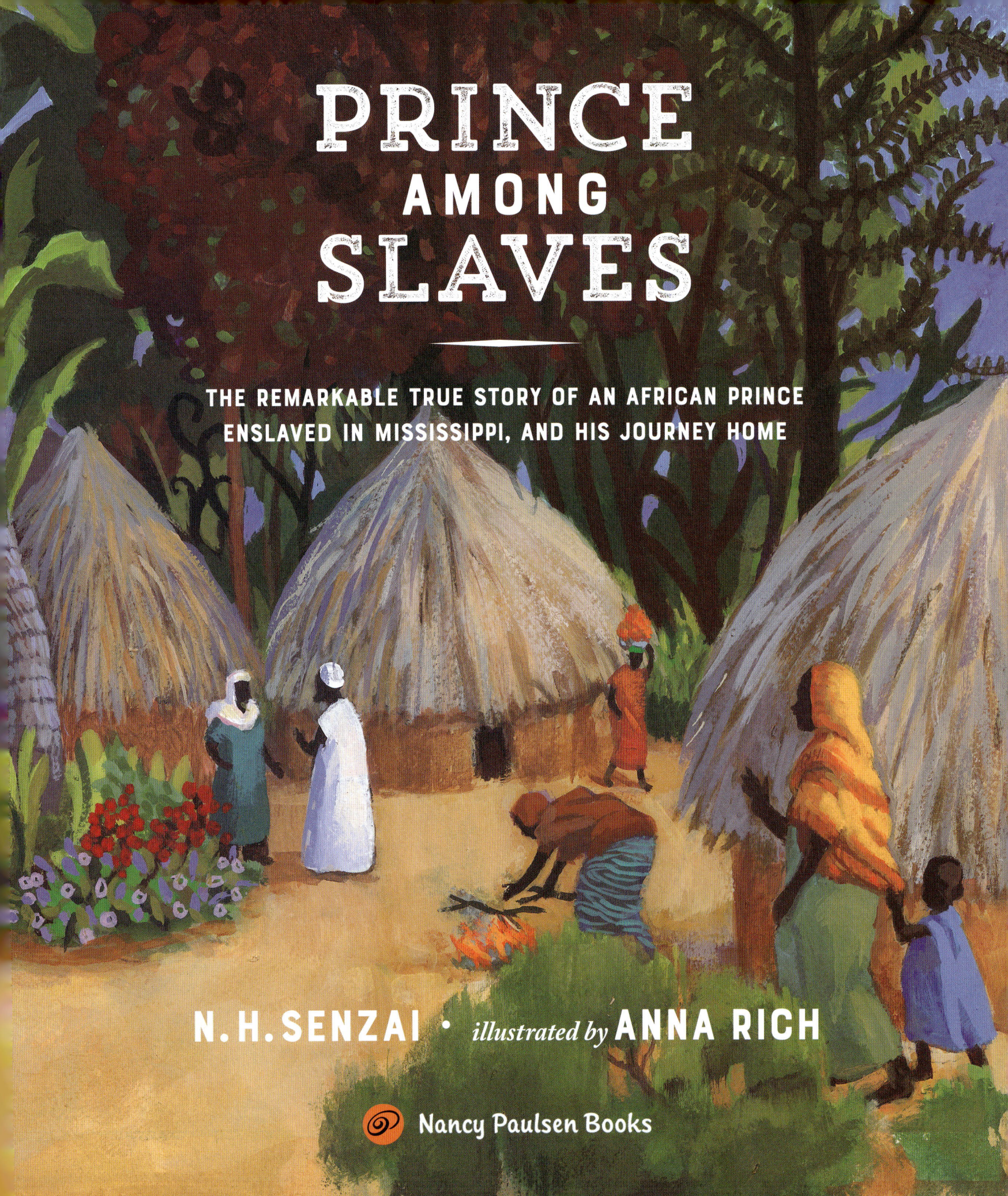

PRINCE AMONG SLAVES

THE REMARKABLE TRUE STORY OF AN AFRICAN PRINCE ENSLAVED IN MISSISSIPPI, AND HIS JOURNEY HOME

N. H. SENZAI • illustrated by ANNA RICH

Nancy Paulsen Books

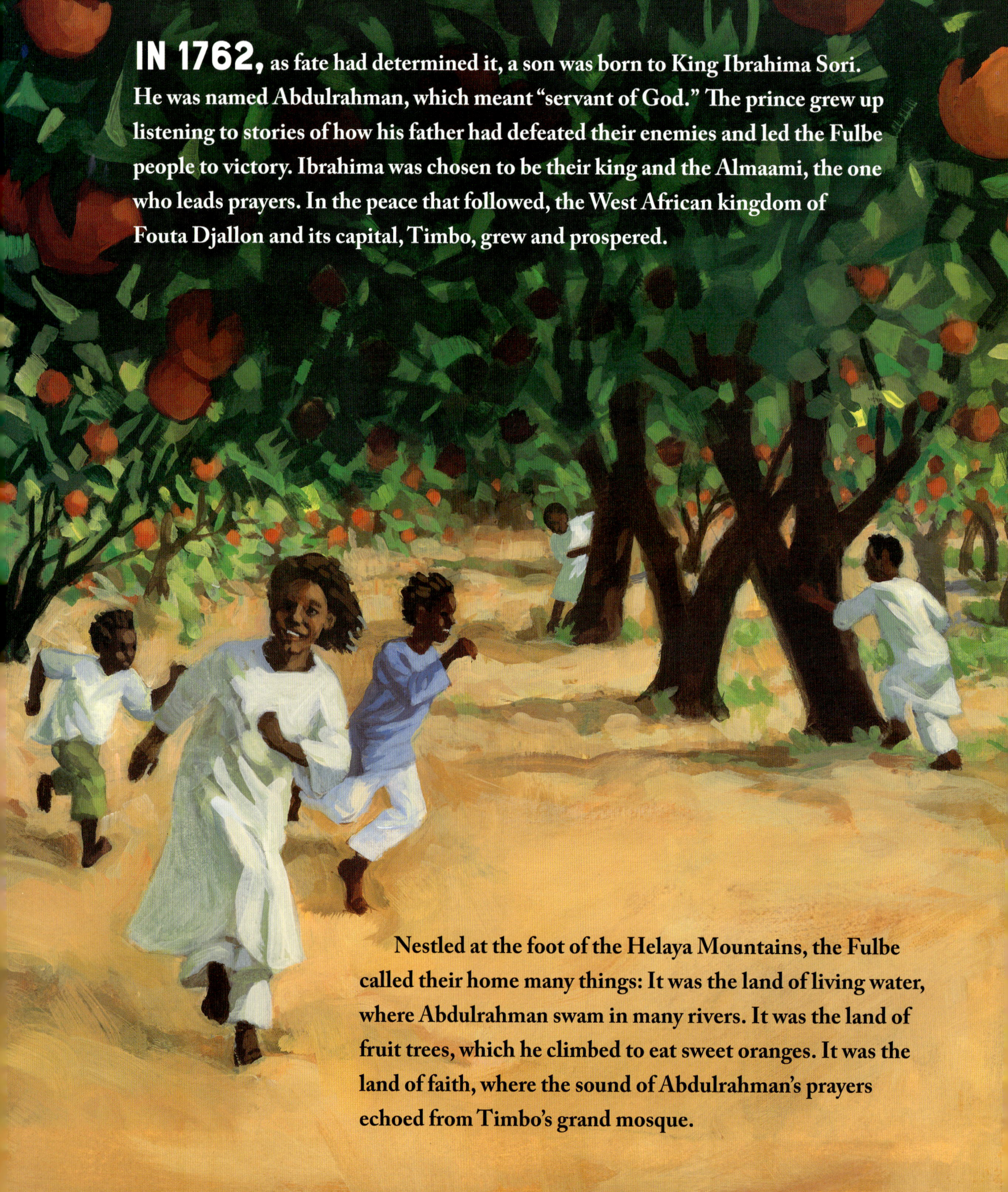

IN 1762, as fate had determined it, a son was born to King Ibrahima Sori. He was named Abdulrahman, which meant "servant of God." The prince grew up listening to stories of how his father had defeated their enemies and led the Fulbe people to victory. Ibrahima was chosen to be their king and the Almaami, the one who leads prayers. In the peace that followed, the West African kingdom of Fouta Djallon and its capital, Timbo, grew and prospered.

Nestled at the foot of the Helaya Mountains, the Fulbe called their home many things: It was the land of living water, where Abdulrahman swam in many rivers. It was the land of fruit trees, which he climbed to eat sweet oranges. It was the land of faith, where the sound of Abdulrahman's prayers echoed from Timbo's grand mosque.

When Abdulrahman turned seven, he was sent to school. Curious and clever, he quickly mastered reading and writing. But what fascinated him most were the stories about the prophets in the holy Quran. Moses, Jesus, and Muhammad had faced great challenges and ordeals. Each had accepted their fate determined by God, no matter how difficult.

Observing his son's intelligence, King Sori sent Abdulrahman to Timbuktu at the age of twelve. Famous for the University of Sankore, built in 989, Timbuktu bustled with scholars, schools, and libraries. Like a parched reed soaking up water, Abdulrahman absorbed lessons of geography, astronomy, calculations, and the law. He became fluent in Arabic and four other African languages. Keeping his faith, he prayed five times a day, facing east, toward Arabia and the holy city of Makkah.

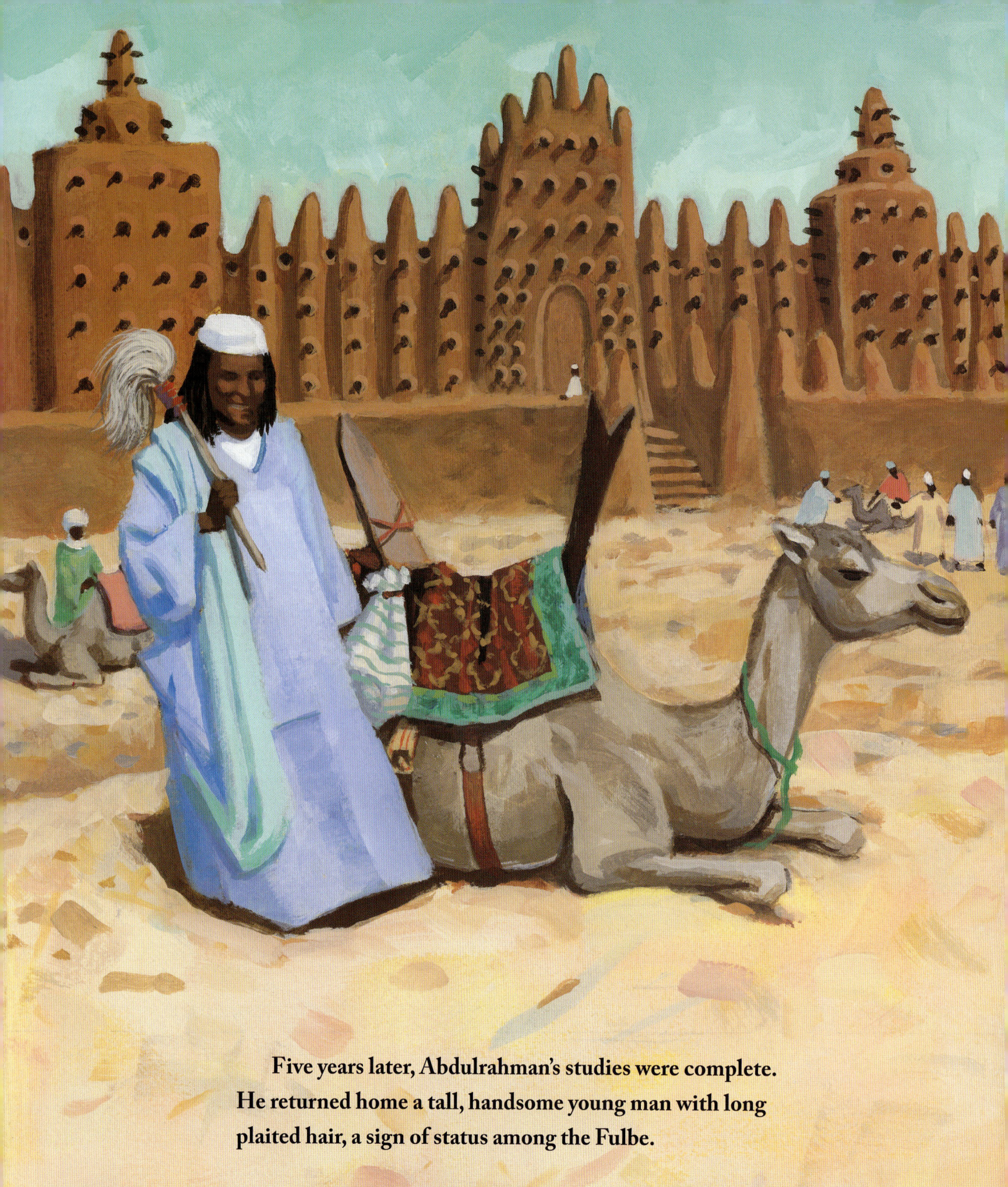

Five years later, Abdulrahman's studies were complete.
He returned home a tall, handsome young man with long
plaited hair, a sign of status among the Fulbe.

He entered the army and began his training as a warrior.

And in his role as prince, he met merchants and diplomats from Africa and across the East at his father's court.

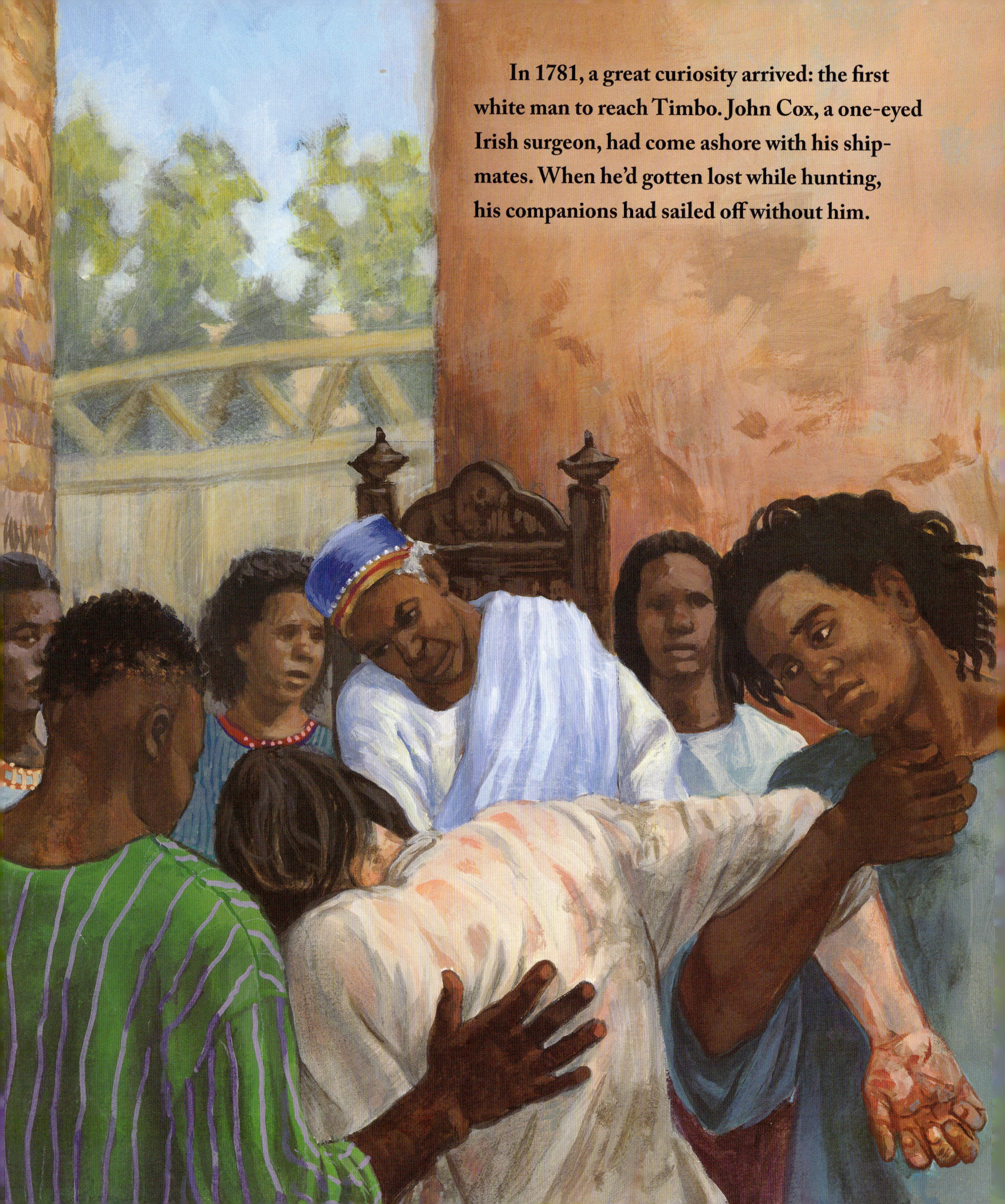

In 1781, a great curiosity arrived: the first white man to reach Timbo. John Cox, a one-eyed Irish surgeon, had come ashore with his shipmates. When he'd gotten lost while hunting, his companions had sailed off without him.

Found sick and injured, King Sori gave the surgeon a house and a nurse and allowed him to stay as long as he wished. Over the next six months, Cox and Abdulrahman spent time together, learned a little of each other's language, and became friends. When Cox became homesick, the king provided guards who took him to the coast, where he boarded a ship back to Ireland.

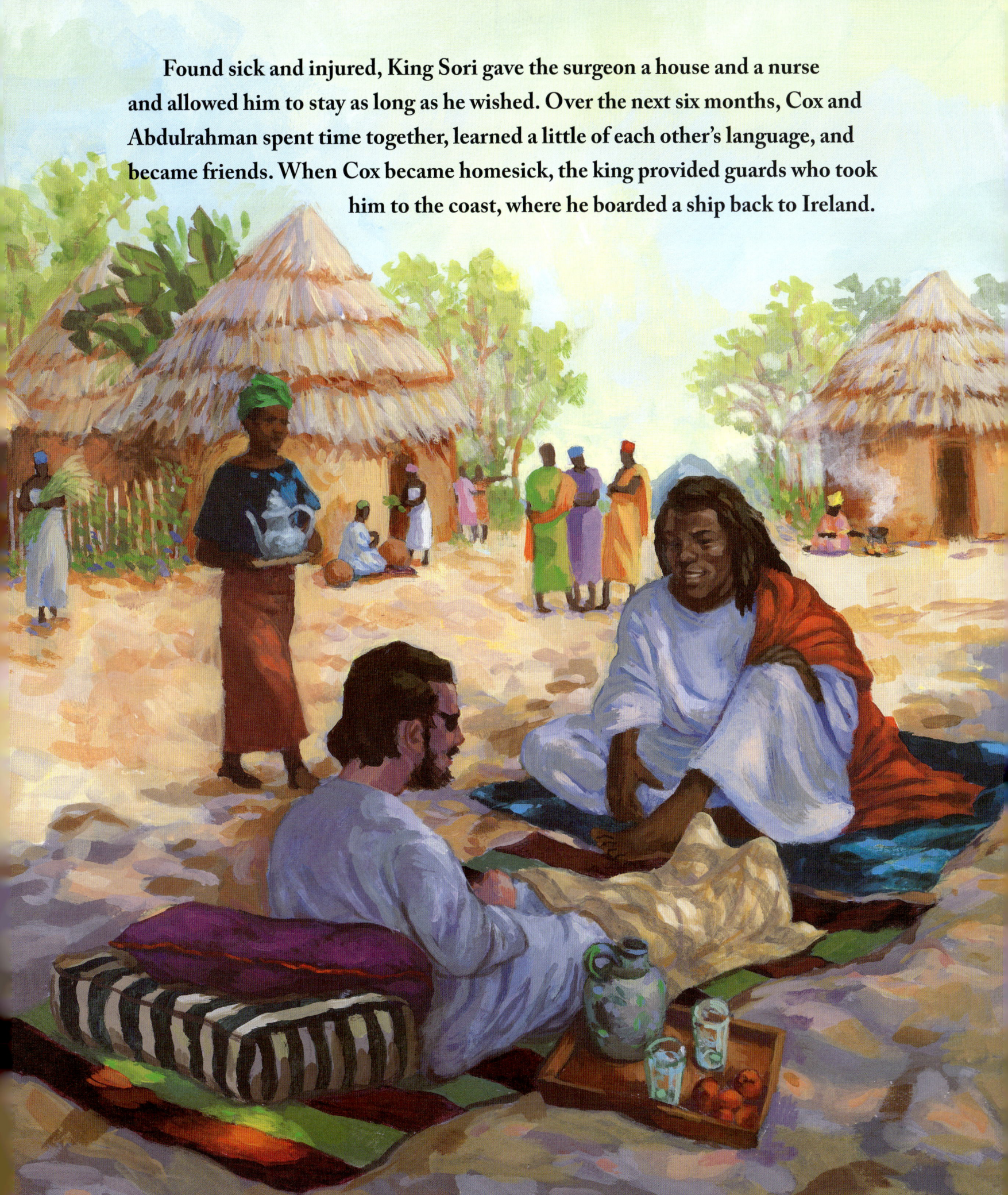

By twenty-six, not only was Abdulrahman a prince destined to be king, he was also a scholar, a warrior, a husband, and the father of a son named Husayn. One day, while on patrol with an army of two thousand soldiers, he was ambushed by the rival Heboh tribe.

Through a haze of bullets, Abdulrahman saw his soldiers drop like rain. One of his men, Samba, came to his aid, and though they fought like lions, they were captured.

Abdulrahman, along with Samba and the other survivors, was marched to the sea. A great ship awaited them, and Abdulrahman was filled with dread. He knew what happened to prisoners of war. They would be sold to English traders who demanded human souls in exchange for gunpowder, muskets, tobacco, and rum.

He struggled and fought at the realization but was beaten and chained. After being dragged on board the ship, called the *Africa*, he was lowered into its dark hold.

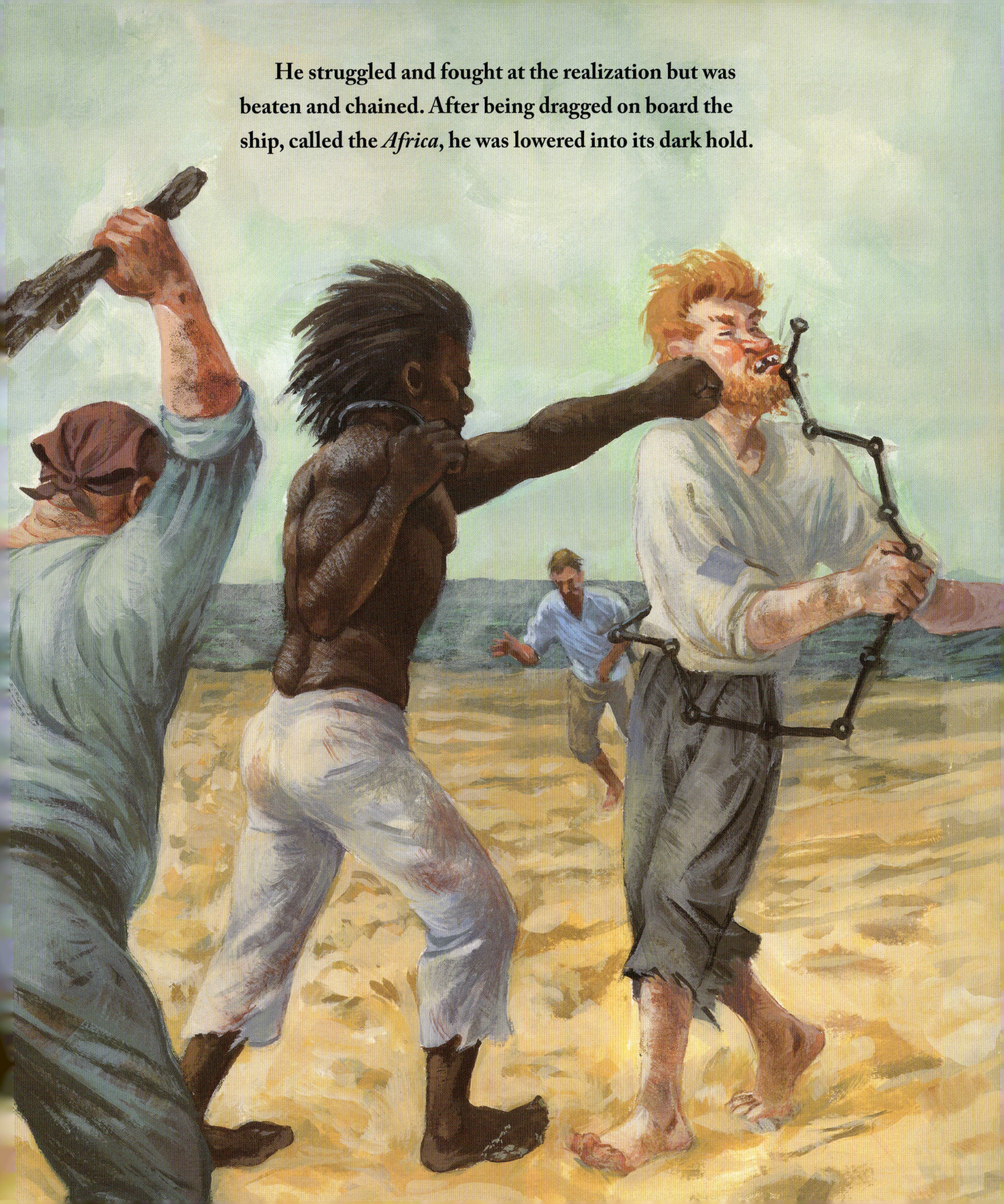

He and 170 others were loaded like cargo into its narrow space.
Men, women, and children, all destined for the same fate—enslavement.
As curses and weeping filled the air, Abdulrahman's own cry
of agony joined the others.

He knew that his father's search parties would be looking
for him. He knew that his mother, his wife, and his son would be
frantic with worry. But he also knew they would not find him.

They journeyed west for eight months, each day filled with misery and grief. Heartbroken, Abdulrahman trembled and raged at being torn from his home.

Brought on deck for a few hours a week, he stood exhausted and powerless. He squeezed his eyes shut as they threw the sick and dying overboard. He could not bear to see the sharks that patrolled the waters, waiting for their next meal.

Three thousand miles they sailed, across the vast expanse of the Atlantic Ocean.

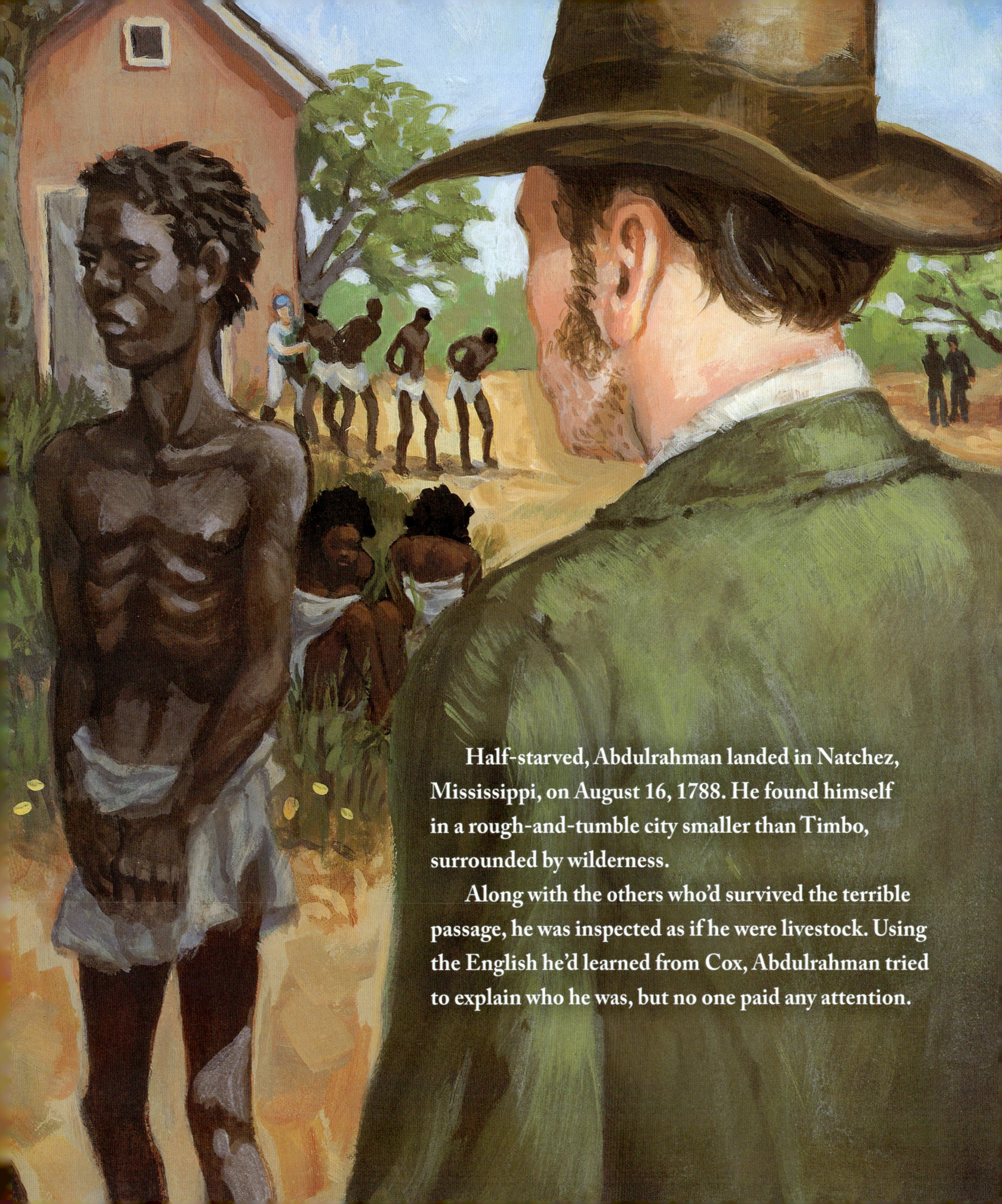

Half-starved, Abdulrahman landed in Natchez, Mississippi, on August 16, 1788. He found himself in a rough-and-tumble city smaller than Timbo, surrounded by wilderness.

Along with the others who'd survived the terrible passage, he was inspected as if he were livestock. Using the English he'd learned from Cox, Abdulrahman tried to explain who he was, but no one paid any attention.

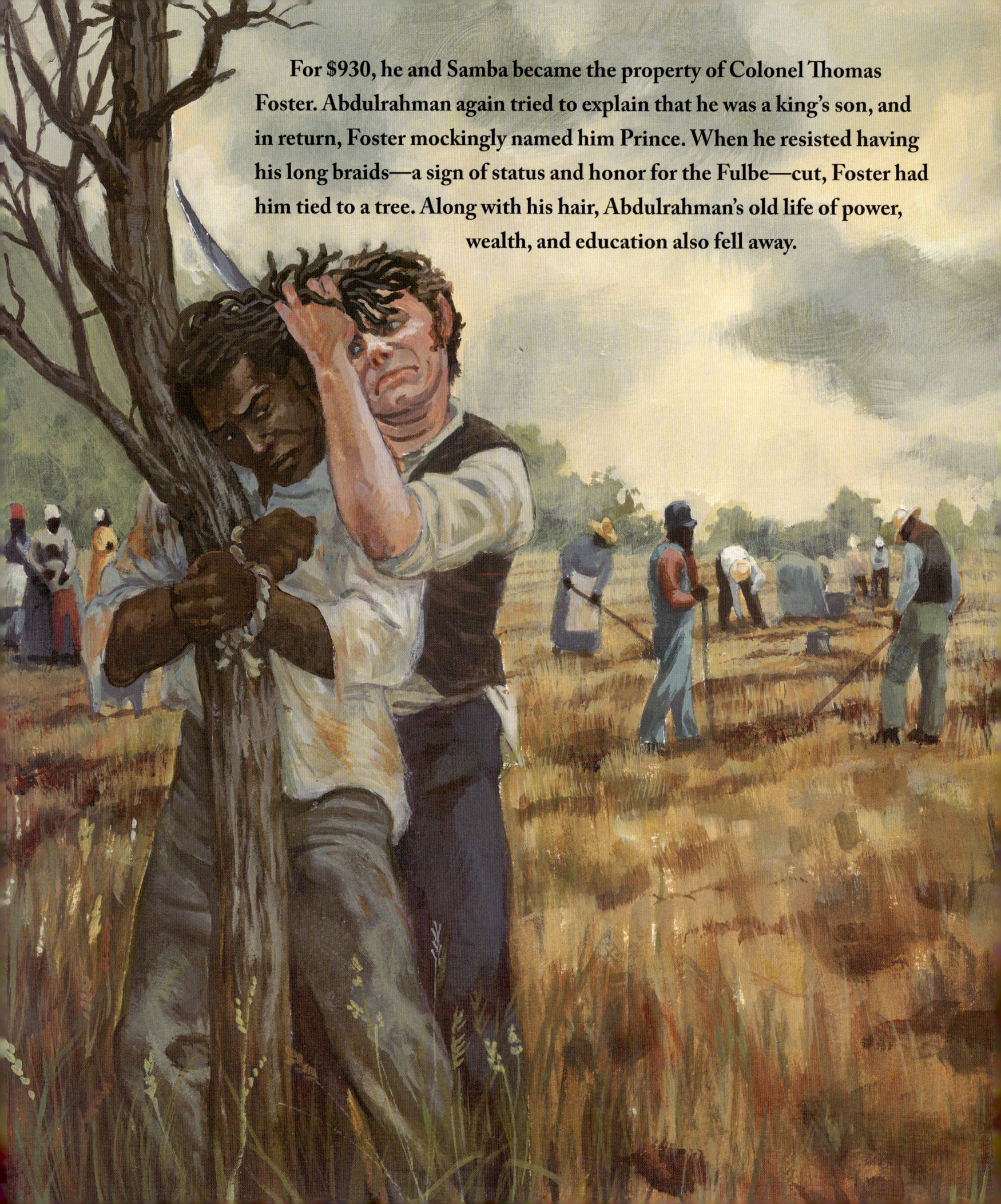

For $930, he and Samba became the property of Colonel Thomas Foster. Abdulrahman again tried to explain that he was a king's son, and in return, Foster mockingly named him Prince. When he resisted having his long braids—a sign of status and honor for the Fulbe—cut, Foster had him tied to a tree. Along with his hair, Abdulrahman's old life of power, wealth, and education also fell away.

Pride and anger burned deep within Abdulrahman, and when Foster ordered him to clear the fields, he refused. After being whipped in punishment, he escaped into the woods.

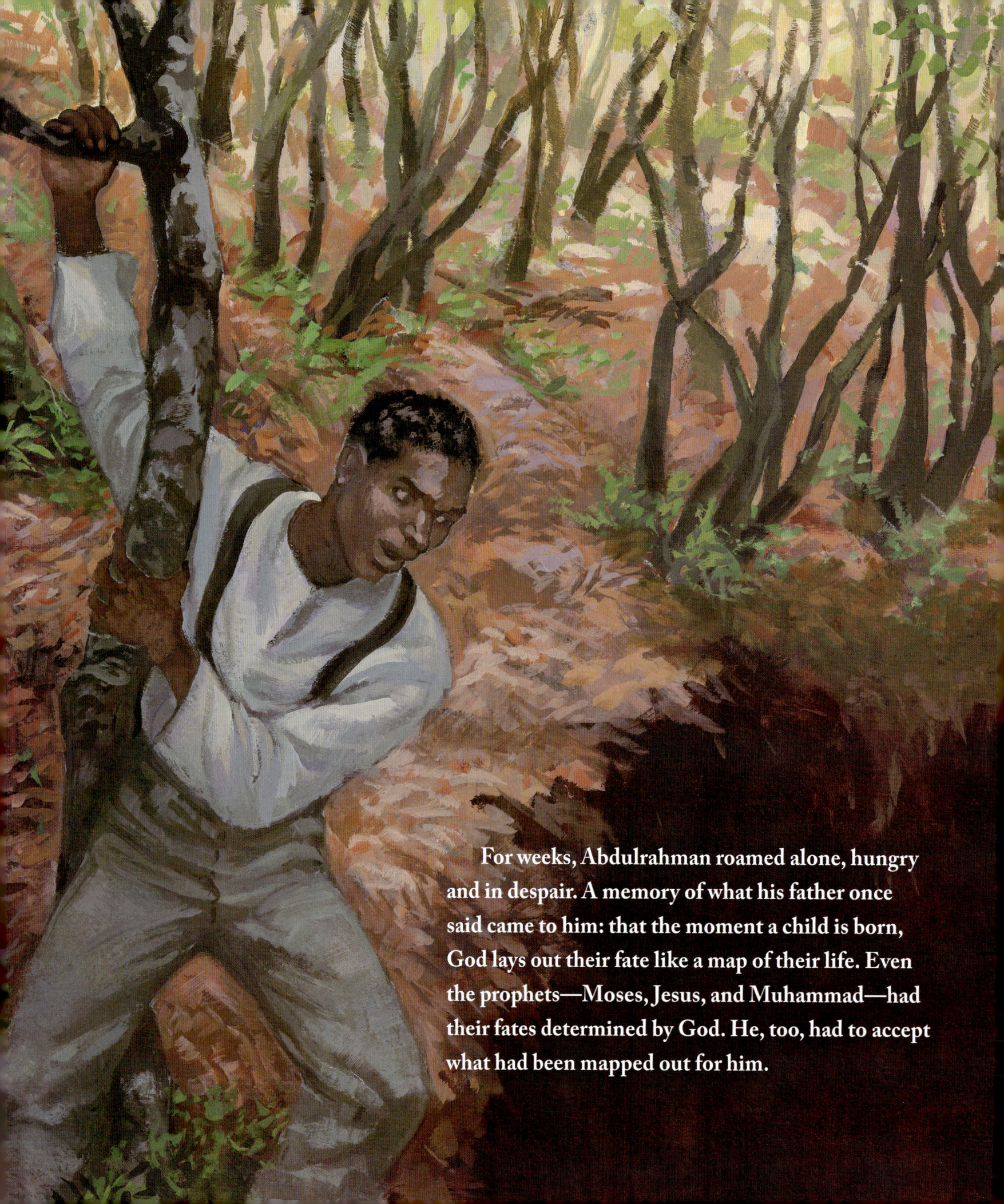

For weeks, Abdulrahman roamed alone, hungry and in despair. A memory of what his father once said came to him: that the moment a child is born, God lays out their fate like a map of their life. Even the prophets—Moses, Jesus, and Muhammad—had their fates determined by God. He, too, had to accept what had been mapped out for him.

Abdulrahman returned and lay down before Foster's astonished wife. He placed her foot on his neck, a sign of submission among the Fulbe. Foster was so relieved to see that his valuable property had returned that he didn't give him the harsh punishment usually given to a runaway slave.

With heavy hearts, both Abdulrahman and Samba realized that return to Fouta Djallon was impossible.

Though not very educated, Foster was an ambitious man. He learned of Abdulrahman's knowledge of cotton, which grew in Fouta Djallon, and with his help, Foster and Abdulrahman grew the crop.

Intelligent, self-disciplined, and resigned to his fate, Abdulrahman proved to be an invaluable worker. He guided Samba and the other enslaved men, who looked to him for leadership. That first year, the farm grew 16,000 pounds of cotton.

Cash in hand, Foster bought more land and slaves, turning the simple farm into a thriving plantation. In return for his loyalty, Foster allowed Abdulrahman to freely practice his faith. This was unusual, since slaveholders traditionally tried to break a slave's connection with their past. In his free time, Abdulrahman could be found facing east in prayer or writing Arabic words in the sand.

On April 15, 1795, five more Africans arrived. One of them was a woman named Isabella. She and Abdulrahman felt a connection, and even though it was risky because they could have been sold away at any moment, they formed a union based on love.

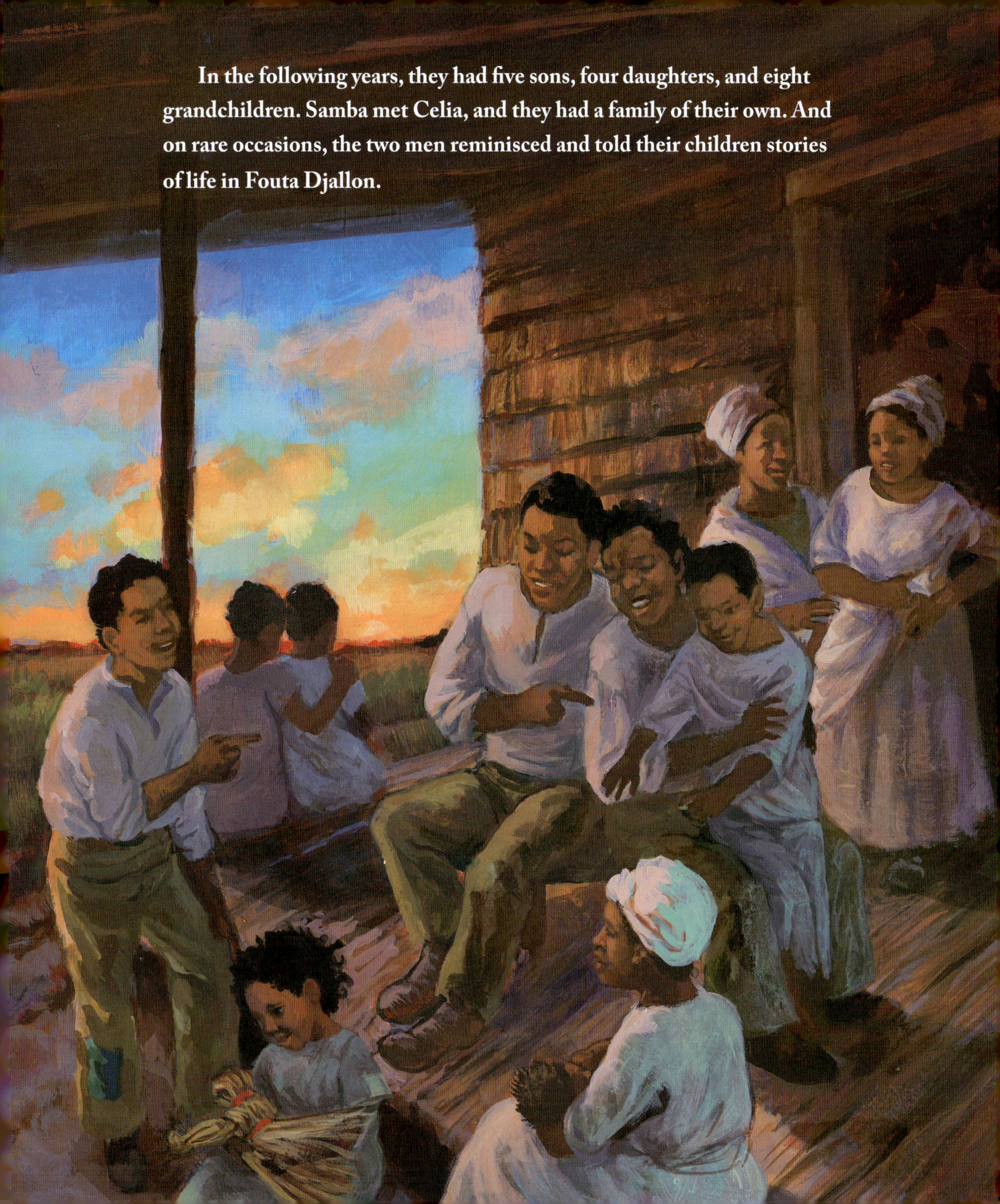

In the following years, they had five sons, four daughters, and eight grandchildren. Samba met Celia, and they had a family of their own. And on rare occasions, the two men reminisced and told their children stories of life in Fouta Djallon.

For his hard work and loyalty, Foster allowed Abdulrahman to sell vegetables at the local market to earn a small income. One Sunday in 1807, a man stopped near his stall. Abdulrahman stared at the man, not quite believing his eyes. It was John Cox, the Irish surgeon who'd been King Sori's guest and Abdulrahman's friend. He had immigrated to the United States from Ireland, settled nearby, and become a respected doctor.

Cox met Foster and explained that Abdulrahman was indeed an African prince and should be set free. Foster, proud that he owned a real prince, one whose labor had made him rich, refused to sell Abdulrahman for any price. The amazing story of the doctor's attempts to free an African prince spread, making them famous.

When the Irishman died nine years later, Samba told Abdulrahman not to despair. God was with those who were steadfast in patience and prayer.

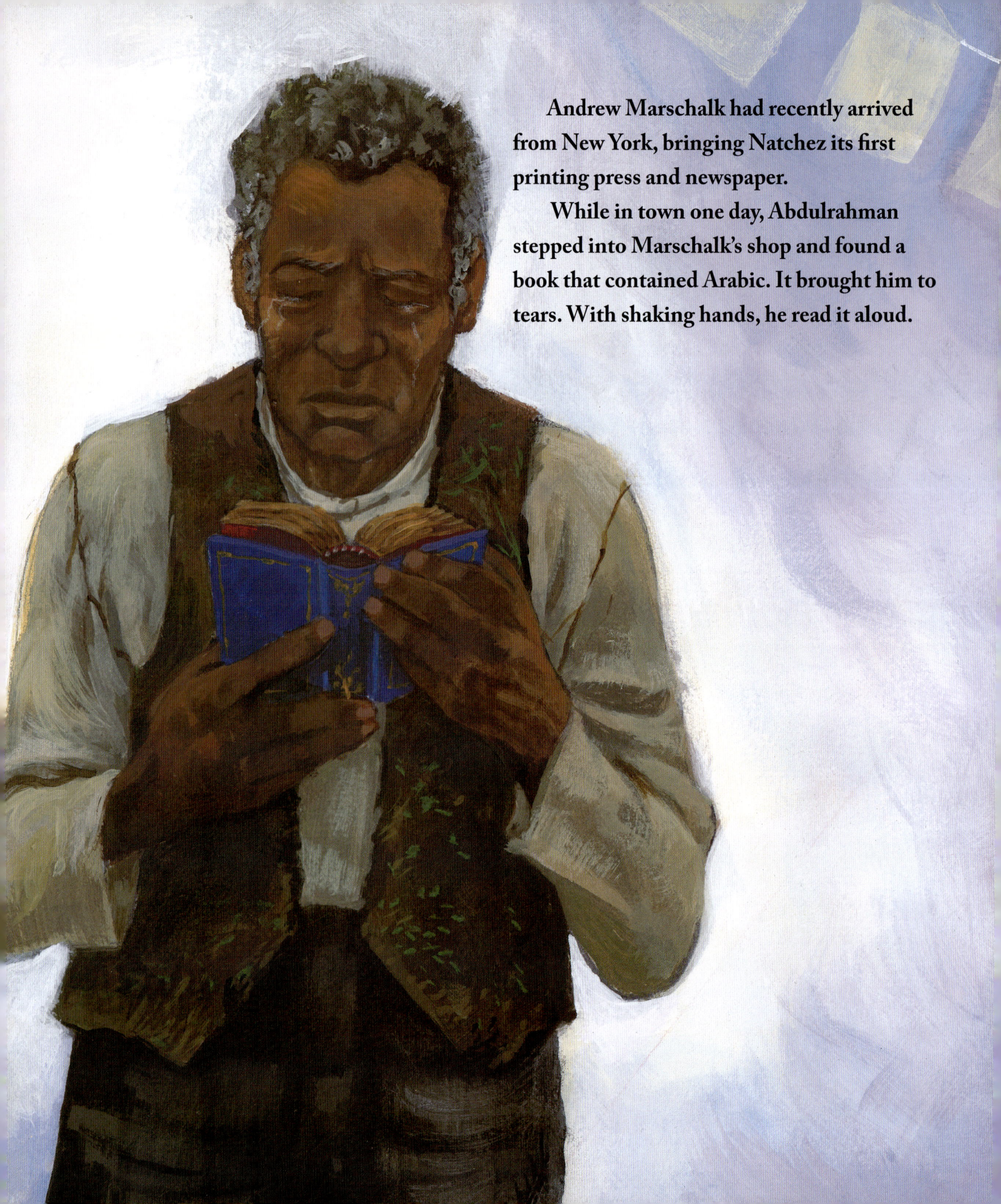

Andrew Marschalk had recently arrived from New York, bringing Natchez its first printing press and newspaper.

While in town one day, Abdulrahman stepped into Marschalk's shop and found a book that contained Arabic. It brought him to tears. With shaking hands, he read it aloud.

Surprised, the printer realized that the stories he'd heard about Abdulrahman were true. And because he was a prince, Marschalk somehow felt that Abdulrahman's enslavement was unjust. He began publishing articles about the well-educated and honorable prince.

Sometimes he stretched the truth, hoping the added color would bring attention to Abdulrahman's plight.

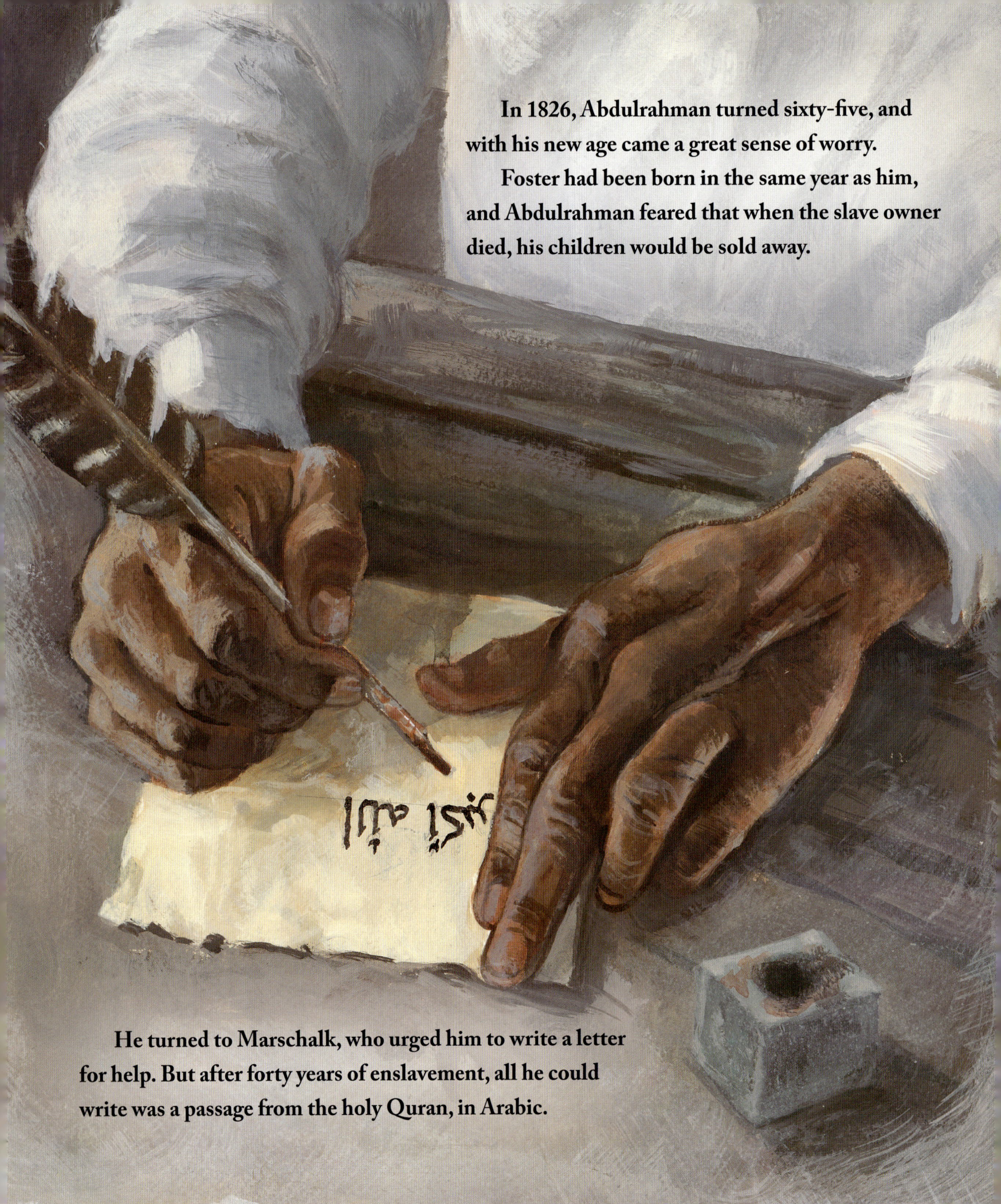

In 1826, Abdulrahman turned sixty-five, and with his new age came a great sense of worry.

Foster had been born in the same year as him, and Abdulrahman feared that when the slave owner died, his children would be sold away.

اللہ اکبر

He turned to Marschalk, who urged him to write a letter for help. But after forty years of enslavement, all he could write was a passage from the holy Quran, in Arabic.

Marschalk gave it to Mississippi senator Thomas Reed, along with a note explaining Abdulrahman's desire to return to Africa. Senator Reed passed it on to Henry Clay, the secretary of state, who then presented it to President John Quincy Adams.

Because it was written in Arabic, they assumed Abdulrahman was an Arab from Morocco, a country in North Africa. President Adams wanted to maintain good relations with Sultan Abd al-Rahman II.

When the sultan saw the letter, he was touched by a fellow Muslim's plight and petitioned for his release. When Abdulrahman learned the amazing news, he kept silent, worried that if Clay and the president learned he was not Moroccan, they would not help him.

Finally, Foster freed Abdulrahman without payment, since he was old and didn't bring much value to the plantation. He had one condition: Abdulrahman could not enjoy the privileges of a free man within the United States. Clay instructed Marschalk to send Abdulrahman to Washington, DC, and from there he would be sent to Morocco.

Joy at the prospect of freedom turned bitter as Abdulrahman thought of leaving his beloved Isabella behind.

When Foster agreed to sell her for $200, Abdulrahman began a campaign in Natchez, requesting donations. Word had spread that the old African, known for his hard work and honesty, was indeed a prince. And after two days, over a hundred people had given him $293 to set Isabella free.

On the plantation that night, Abdulrahman faced east in prayer. For four decades he'd toiled on Foster's fields. Now God had determined that he should be free, but the price was very steep. For the second time in his life, he was leaving behind his family and friends, including Samba, his loyal companion.

Abdulrahman embraced his children and made them a promise. He would do all he could to buy their freedom.

The morning of the couple's departure was clear and calm, but their hearts were filled with agony.

As they sailed up the Mississippi River, Abdulrahman wore the costume of a Moroccan prince. It had been given to him by Marschalk, whose articles had already made him famous. Abdulrahman hoped the outfit would bring more attention so that he could talk about the evils of slavery and hopefully raise funds for his children.

Their first stop was Cincinnati, Ohio, where slavery was outlawed. A free man for the first time in forty years, Abdulrahman attended events held in his honor. He spoke about his life as a slave and collected donations to emancipate his children. On their journey east, newspapers headlined his prince-to-slave story, and Abdulrahman spoke at every opportunity. By the time he arrived in Washington, DC, on May 15, 1828, he was the most famous African in the United States.

President Adams welcomed Abdulrahman to the White House and asked about his journey to Morocco. Finally, Abdulrahman was forced to admit the truth—he was not an Arab from Morocco, but an African returning to Fouta Djallon. The president's support cooled, and he did not offer aid to help free his children as Abdulrahman had hoped.

Deeply disappointed, Abdulrahman turned to the American Colonization Society, led by Thomas Gallaudet. The society had established the colony of Liberia in West Africa to resettle free Blacks. Gallaudet offered help, believing Abdulrahman to be a Christian, hoping to use his fame for the society's cause. Again, Abdulrahman kept silent for the sake of his children.

After ten months of delays to raise funds for his children, Abdulrahman's health began to decline. In a final effort, he traveled to Boston, where he was invited to speak at the African Masonic Lodge. Abdulrahman gave an impassioned speech about the ills of slavery, bringing those in attendance to cheer and cry. He collected some money, but not nearly enough to free his children.

Back in Natchez, reports of Abdulrahman's fame angered slave owners. They felt he was stirring up racial trouble with his speeches against slavery. Foster declared the government had violated their agreement. He threatened to enslave Abdulrahman again and refused to free his children.

Abdulrahman knew he could no longer stay in the United States—it was too dangerous. With a heavy heart, he and Isabella boarded the *Harriet*, a ship chartered by the American Colonization Society. In its finest cabin, they headed east, traveling the same waters that had brought him to Natchez.

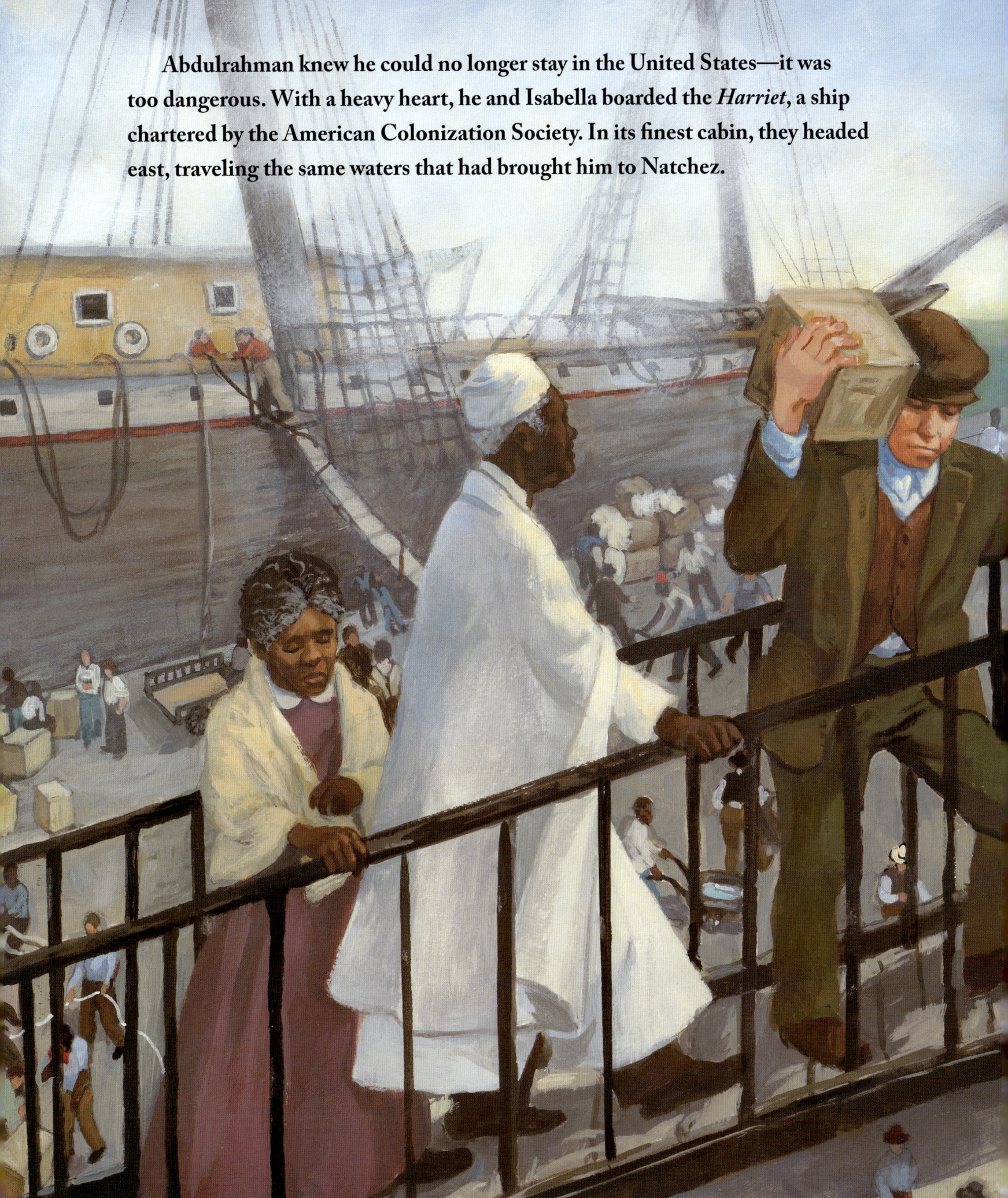

On March 18, 1829, Abdulrahman stepped ashore in Monrovia, Liberia, and knelt in prayer. Next, he sent a letter to his friends, informing them of his arrival, and asked their help to free his children. He had escaped the shackles of slavery and returned to the continent of his birth, a feat very few achieved, but his return was bittersweet.

After four months of waiting and hoping that his sons would arrive, he died from fever at the age of sixty-seven. As fate had determined it, he never reached Fouta Djallon or saw his beloved children again. Foster died that same year, and Abdulrahman's friends were able to buy the freedom of two of his sons. They, along with their families, were reunited with Isabella in Liberia.

One hundred and seventy-seven years later, in 2006, an extraordinary event took place on Foster's field: Abdulrahman's descendants gathered for a reunion, bringing together the African and American branches of the family. Long after Abdulrahman's death, his dream was finally fulfilled.

AUTHOR'S NOTE

I FIRST ENCOUNTERED Abdulrahman's story in Unity Productions Foundation's wonderful film, produced by Michael Wolfe and Alex Kronemer. What struck me deeply about Abdulrahman was his resilience and strength of character as he dealt with the horrors of enslavement and the loss of his family and homeland. Searching for more, I found his biography written by Terry Alford. In 1968, while doing research for his PhD in American history, in the archives of the Natchez, Mississippi, courthouse, Professor Alford found a letter dated January 12, 1828. Signed by Henry Clay, secretary of state, it was addressed to the sultan of Morocco, the first country to formally recognize the United States after its independence in 1777. The letter concerned the freeing of an enslaved man who was said to be a "Moorish" prince.

The more I learned about Abdulrahman, the more I knew I had to share his story for a younger audience. Although I am not from Africa nor a man, I felt connected to him through faith—as a Muslim, I understood how he submitted to the will of Allah and accepted the path set before him. I was in awe of how Abdulrahman navigated the reality of enslavement and built a life for himself and his family with such incredible dignity.

Having studied the work of scholars like the late Dr. Sulayman Nyang, chair of the African Studies Department at Howard University, I knew Abdulrahman was not a rarity. Dr. Nyang had found that up to 30 percent of enslaved Africans came from Islamic regions, which today are the nations of Senegal, Mali, Guinea, Sierra Leone, and Gambia. Other well-known Muslims enslaved during the early 1800s were Bilali Muhammad, Fatima, Yarrow Mamout, Mandinka Jeanne, and Omar ibn Said, an Islamic scholar whose memoir is the basis of a Pulitzer Prize–winning opera called *Omar*.

Islam has been part of America's landscape since its founding, and enslaved Muslim men and women strove to keep their faith and follow the fate Allah had laid for them. Abdulrahman resisted subjugation by living the best life he could, but when the opportunity for freedom arrived in 1829, he seized it. Between the ban of the transatlantic slave trade in 1808 and the Emancipation Proclamation in 1863, it was a violent, tumultuous time among those committed to slavery and those who desired its abolition. Abdulrahman never expected to be free or return home, but he took tremendous risks speaking about the ills of slavery to raise money to free his children. His fiery speeches and the media attention they drew nearly returned him to the shackles of slavery.

My hope is that Abdulrahman's story resonates with readers and illustrates how Muslims have historically been an integral part of the American narrative. His life provides a new lens through which to view how those stolen from Africa survived enslavement and the impact those souls made on our collective history. I feel this is even more important as we look at the current landscape of our nation, where forces still strive to silence stories through book bans and limit the teaching of American history. Abdulrahman's extraordinary legacy has taught me to commit to the fate laid out before me by Allah, be judicious, and strive for justice by taking risks in doing what's right for myself, my family, my community, and my nation. ⋍

A book comes to life through many hands, and Abdulrahman's story is no different. I'd like to thank my long-supporting agent, Michael Bourret; the incredible illustrator who gave the characters color, Anna Rich; my editor, to whom I feel I am returning, Stacey Barney; visionary art directors Eileen Savage and Marikka Tamura; designer Suki Boynton; and the extraordinary team at Nancy Paulsen Books.